SNOWDONIA
MOODS

Jerry Rawson

HALSGROVE

First published in Great Britain in 2004

Title page photograph: The afterglow of the setting sun has created a moody atmosphere in this shot of the sea and boulders near Llanbedr, with the Lleyn Peninsula on the distant horizon.

British Library Cataloguing-in-Publication Data
A CIP record for this title is available from the British Library

ISBN 1 84114 385 5

HALSGROVE
Halsgrove House
Lower Moor Way
Tiverton, Devon EX16 6SS
Tel: 01884 243242
Fax: 01884 243325
email: sales@halsgrove.com
website: www.halsgrove.com

Printed and bound by D'Auria Industrie Grafiche Spa, Italy

INTRODUCTION

The Snowdonia National Park – *Parc Cenedlaethol Eryri* in Welsh – was designated as a National Park in 1951, and lies in the north-west corner of Wales. It contains some of the most spectacular and tightly-packed mountain scenery in the United Kingdom.

It is a land of heather moors, lakes, wooded valleys, rivers, waterfalls, and brooding, craggy, mountain ranges. Within the boundary of the 827 square miles (2142 sq km) of the National Park there are 23 miles (37 km) of coastline with beaches, sand dunes, and great sweeping bays, such as Tremadog and Mawddach. This means that it is difficult to escape the sea, and from many mountain tops you can catch glimpses of it.

It is the rocks (some of the oldest in the world), earth movements, and erosion, which have combined to create the many facets of Snowdonia. But the final shaping of the landscape we see today was brought about relatively recently during the Ice Age. Glaciers only disappeared about 10,000 years ago.

Humans have also influenced the landscape we see today, stretching back over 6000 years from when Neolithic people started to settle and farm here, through the Bronze and Iron Ages, the Roman occupation, and the Middle Ages, up to the present day.

Sheep farming, mining for minerals and slate quarrying have all left their marks on the landscape during the last few centuries. Some slate quarrying still exists, albeit on a smaller scale, and although many of the relics from mining and quarrying still remain, nature is steadily reclaiming the ruins which are still a fascinating feature of many parts of Snowdonia.

Snowdonia offers great opportunities to landscape photographers and each season has its own beauty, from the colourful display of wild flowers in the Conwy Valley during springtime; the purple-clad heather moors above Bala in high summer; the golden autumnal colours of the ancient woods around Dolgellau; to the vast Arctic-like winter plateau of the Carneddau, the rugged Glyderau and especially majestic Snowdon (Yr Wyddfa), at 1085 m/3560 feet, the highest summit in England and Wales. All these bristling summits look especially spectacular when cloaked in snow.

Chasing the light across this precious landscape can be very rewarding, but it also requires great patience. You can be sitting on the top of a hill waiting for the sun to rise, only to find a bank of cloud rolling in from the east blocking out the magical dawn light. Or sheltering behind rocks waiting for heavy rain to pass over and, you hope, leave storm clouds and dramatic light. The best photographic conditions are often around dawn and dusk when the light can be a revelation, transforming a mundane landscape into something quite sublime.

The choice of pictures and their order is purely personal, as we take a photographic odyssey from north to south, capturing the energy and moods of the Snowdonia landscape throughout all the seasons. We start at the Carneddau, then explore the rocky cwms and soaring ridges of Tryfan and the Glyderau, then the craggy ramparts of Snowdon beckon, before the grassy hills of the Nantlle ridge are visited. In marked contrast, our photographic journey then continues to the quieter Cnicht and Moelwyn hills, the wooded areas around Bala and Dolgellau, the rocky ridges of the Rhinogydd, and the coastal areas to the west, finally visiting the impressive southern sentinel of Cadair Idris, with its broad ridges and hanging cwms.

Hopefully the choice of photographs has captured the beauty and atmosphere of this precious landscape, and maybe they will encourage readers to go and discover the area for themselves. I apologise if your favourite place has been left out.

Jerry Rawson

LOCATION MAP – Showing National Park Boundary

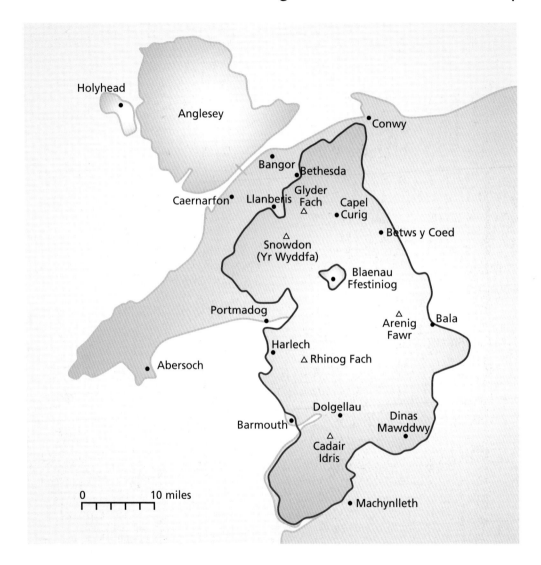

AUTHOR'S ACKNOWLEDGEMENTS

I would like to acknowledge the help and support from my wife Katy Rawson with proof reading, artwork and map and also Roly Smith, editorial manager for Halsgrove and president of the Outdoor Writers' Guild, for his guidance and editorial help.

Left: The cascades of Rhaeadr-fawr – usually known as Aber Falls – on the northern slopes of the Carneddau near Abergwyngregyn.

Previous page: The first light of a cold winter's dawn adds a rosy-pink hue to the Snowdon hills.

A carpet of bluebells adds colour to this woodland scene near Aber.

Storms sweep across Llyn Eigiau, situated in the remote eastern section of the Carneddau.

A track draws the eye to an isolated
dwelling in the remote Cwm Eigiau,
in the Carneddau.

Boulders create an interesting foreground for this view of Craig yr Ysfa and Pen yr Helgi Du
seen from the slopes of Carnedd Llewelyn in the Carneddau.

Early morning sunshine on the wind-blown surface of Ffynnon Llugwy Reservoir
seen here from the slopes of Craig yr Ysfa in the Carneddau.

A passing snow shower dusts the summit of Pen Llithrig y Wrach in the eastern Carneddau.

Mist swirls around the shapely peak of Elidir Fawr in this view across the Nant Ffrancon from the summit slopes of Pen yr Ole Wen.

The shapely peak of Tryfan dominates this late afternoon view across Llyn Ogwen from Pen yr Ole Wen.
The ridge lit up on the right of Tryfan is Y Gribin, an airy approach to the summit of Glyder Fawr.

Storm clouds sweep across Snowdonia. The dramatic light gives the scene atmosphere and mood.

A combination of water, rocks
and trees in this view of a stream
meandering through the rocky gorge
of Fairy Glen near Betws y Coed.

The Afon Llugwy, swollen by overnight rain, flows through Capel Curig before passing under a bridge where it plunges over the Cyfyng Falls.

Autumn leaves are highlighted as the Afon Llugwy flows silkily around a mossy boulder.

Grasses silhouetted by the setting sun.

The cascades of Rhaedr Ogwen (Ogwen Falls) provide a foreground for this view of Foel-goch.

An early morning view of Y Garn and Foel-goch reflected in the calm waters of Llyn Ogwen.

Opposite: The outflow from Llyn Ogwen backed by Tryfan.

Right: The same viewpoint as opposite, when a break during a snowstorm allows sunshine to pick out Tryfan, in this bleak monochrome scene by Llyn Ogwen.

Above: A patch of sunshine breaks through summer rain clouds to pick out Llyn Ogwen in this view along the Ogwen Valley.

Opposite: Vibrant purple heather adds colour to this summer scene of a stream rushing down the slopes from Llyn Idwal.

Early morning light brightens the impressive rocky buttresses and ridges on the east face of Tryfan, whose pyramid shape dominates this classic view through the Ogwen Valley.

Crags ring the top of Tryfan's north summit.

The grasses on the
edge of Llyn Idwal act
as a foreground for this
view of Y Garn.

The same view from Llyn Idwal to
Y Garn as opposite, but this
time after a heavy snowfall.

The lingering light of a summer evening picks out the summit slopes of Pen yr Ole Wen, reflected in Llyn Idwal.

A glacial erratic boulder is used as a foreground for this view into the impressive glacier-carved Cwm Idwal, with the cleft of Twll Du (Devil's Kitchen), visible in the craggy head wall of the cwm.

Sunshine highlights the sweep of Idwal Slabs on the flanks of Glyder Fawr.
These easy-angled slabs have been a playground for generations of rock climbers.

Cwm Idwal is redolent with the history of Welsh rock climbing. Here, a climber balances his way up Suicide Wall on the East Wall of Cwm Idwal, with Llyn Idwal in the background.

Tryfan reflected in the waters of a tiny lake, often dry in summer, situated below the craggy east face of Glyder Fach.

A scrambler in an exposed position
on the spectacular pinnacled ridge
of Cneifion Arete in Cwm Cneifion –
often known as the Nameless Cwm
– tucked above Cwm Idwal.

Gylder Fach reflected in Llyn y Caseg-fraith. The pinnacled Bristly Ridge is visible on the right skyline.

Walkers crossing the pinnacles on Bristly Ridge, an exciting approach to the summit of Glyder Fach. Llyn Ogwen is visible in the background.

Tryfan reflected in the mirror-like surface of Llyn y Caseg-fraith situated on the east ridge of Glyder Fach.

An early morning view of the east face of Tryfan, and its neighbour Glyder Fach,
seen across Cwm Tryfan from the ridge of Braich y Ddeugwm.

Above: A sunlit boulder reflects the shape of Tryfan, backed by the Carneddau,
in this view from the upper slopes of Glyder Fach.

Opposite: The rocks at the top of Y Gribin, a ridge on Glyder Fach, lead the eye across Llyn Idwal to Y Garn
backed by Foel-goch, with the trench of Nant Francon, a classic glacial trough, on the right.

Above: The splintered crest of Castell y Gwynt (Castle of the Winds) backed by Glyder Fawr and the Snowdon range.

Opposite: Erosion by wind and rain has created this remarkable cluster of rocks
on the summit slopes of Glyder Fawr. Y Garn in the background.

Fangs of rock covered in rime ice, near
the summit of Glyder Fawr.

The summit slopes of Y Garn reflected in Llyn y Cwn, a small lake situated in a hollow overlooking the Devil's Kitchen in Cwm Idwal.

The lovely Llyn Bochlwyd, situated in a rocky hollow below the north slopes of Glyder Fach.

A misty autumn morning by Llyn Padarn.

A summer's evening by Llyn Padarn near Llanberis, with the Snowdon range mirrored in the calm water.

Evening sunshine picks out a lone tree, to create a dramatic image across the Llanberis Pass to Cwm Glas Mawr.

A broken wall leads to the old farm
of Ynys Ettws in the Llanberis Pass,
overlooked by Cwm Glas Mawr,
swathed in veils of mist.

Sunshine illuminates the craggy Dinas Mot, backed by Cwm Glas Mawr and Crib Goch high above the Llanberis Pass.

The Snowdon hills in their winter blanket reflected in Llynnau Mymbyr, near Capel Curig. A classic view of Snowdon.

The sun sets beyond the Snowdon hills in this view across Llynnau Mymbyr, near Capel Curig.

Y Lliwedd reflected in Llyn Teyrn,
seen from the Miners' Track approach
to Snowdon (Yr Wyddfa)
via Pen y Pass.

Walkers ascending the narrow ridge connecting Crib Goch with Crib y Ddysgl, seen across the upper reaches of Cwm Uchaf.

The pyramid-shaped Snowdon (Yr Wyddfa)
soaring above the turquoise-coloured waters
of Glaslyn, with the Crib Goch pinnacles
in the foreground.

A lone walker adds scale to this view of the Crib Goch pinnacles backed by the
narrow ridge sweeping up to the summit of Crib y Ddysgl.

Veils of mist swirl around the summits of Snowdon (Yr Wyddfa) and Crib Goch,
which in conditions like these look almost like Himalayan giants.

Snowdon (Yr Wyddfa) lit by early morning sunshine. The sunlit rocky ridge of Cribau provides
an exciting scrambling approach to Yr Wyddfa from Glaslyn.

Shades of white, high on the slopes of Crib y Ddysgl.

The east face of Snowdon (Yr Wyddfa) topped by the railway terminus. When covered in snow, this face provides a popular venue for snow and ice climbers.

A sea of mist washes against the southern ridge of Snowdon (Yr Wyddfa) in this evening view from the summit.

The craggy peak of Y Lliwedd
dressed in its icy shawl.

Early morning sunshine illuminates the summit ridge of Y Lliwedd backed by Snowdon (Yr Wyddfa).

The rounded, grassy Moel Eilio, which overlooks Llanberis, is seen in this view across
Cwm Dwythwch, from the slopes of Moel Cynghorion.

Left: Cascades on the Afon Hwch situated on the lower slopes of Moel Eilio.

Opposite: The Afon Glaslyn tumbles down the hillside below the mist-shrouded Cwm Dyli on the eastern flanks of Snowdon (Yr Wyddfa).

A solitary tree acts as a focal point in this winter view across Nant Gwynant to Crib Goch.

The Snowdon Horseshoe – a challenging winter expedition for walkers – seen in its full glory stretching from Crib Goch to Y Lliwedd.

Transparent ice coats stream-side grasses.

The last rays of evening sunshine catch the summit slopes of Moel Hebog in this view across Llyn Gwynant.

Fluffy clouds drift over the isolated and shapely peak of Yr Aran, an outlier
on the south ridge of Snowdon, seen across Llyn Gwynant.

A vibrant mix of early autumn
colours add charm to this view of
the deep narrow gorge of the
Pass of Aberglaslyn, near Beddgelert.

A stream from Llyn Llagi
to the north-west of
Cnicht flows gently down
to join the Nanmor, with
the Snowdon range in
the background across
Nant Gwynant.

Two fishermens' boats beside Llyn y Dywarchen near Rhyd-Ddu. Snowdon and its western cwms dominate the skyline ahead.

Rocks and winter grasses act as a foreground in this view south-west, from Llyn y Dywarchen, to the distant pointed peak of Yr Aran.

A snow-dusted Mynydd Mawr, and the rocky ridges of Craig y Bera,
situated high above the Nantlle Valley.

Y Garn, and Mynydd Mawr (on the right), after a sudden snow shower, seen from near the village of Rhyd-Ddu.

The Nantlle Ridge, one of the finest ridges in Snowdonia, sweeps south-west from Y Garn.

A walker on the narrow rocky ridge leading to the summit of Mynydd Drws y Coed, on the Nantlle Ridge.

The craggy buttresses on the northern flanks of Craig Cwm Silyn on the Nantlle Ridge, seen here across Llynnau Cwm Silyn.

A fern adds a touch of colour to this slate wall near Blaenau Ffestiniog.

Relics of slate quarrying in Cwm Orthin, seen across Llyn Cwmorthin, above Tanygrisiau, just west of Blaenau Ffestiniog.

Left: A foxglove blooms amongst the slate tips.

Opposite: The decaying ruins slowly being reclaimed by nature are a reminder of the slate-quarrying days in Cwm Orthin.

Above: Cotton grass silhouetted against the setting sun.

Opposite: Slate fences line up like tombstones at the disused Rhosydd slate quarry, on the high pass between Blaenau Ffestiniog and Croeser.

An isolated white house with the craggy hill of Moel-ddu in the background, seen from the road to the village of Croesor.

A farmstead in Cwm Croesor backed by the Nantlle hills.

Right: The shapely peak of Cnicht rising above Croesor. Though often known as the Matterhorn of Wales, this elegant peak, when viewed from the west, is really the end of a long ridge.

Opposite: Croesor, a village forever associated with the slate industry, which has formed such an integral part of the history and heritage of this region. The hill in the background is Moel Hebog.

Looking from Moelwyn Mawr over the ridge of Craigysgafn to Moelwyn Bach, which overlook Blaenau Ffestiniog. The walkers add scale to this grey mountain landscape.

Oxeye daisies.

Pistyll Rhaerdr – one of the traditional wonders of Wales – in the Berwyn hills, to the north-east of Llangynog. The waters of the Afon Disgynfa drop 245 feet (75m) in two fine cascades.

Low evening sunlight casts long shadows across the hillside near Llangynog, the Berwyn hills.

Storm clouds sweep over Moel Sych and, on the right, the pointed hill of Cadair Berwyn.

A feast of autumn foliage.

A mixture of leaves create an attractive mosaic of colours on the woodland floor.

A patchwork of autumn colours reflected in the calm waters of Llyn Tegid near Bala.

Stormy sunset over Llyn Tegid, Bala.

Misty morning on Llyn Tegid looking south to Aran Benllyn.

Early morning light illuminates this eastern view from the north ridge of
Aran Benllyn to the distant hills of Moel Llyfnant and Arenig Fawr.

Looking east from Aran Fawddwy to the distant rolling hills of the Berwyn.

Snowdrops herald the arrival of spring
in this woodland scene.

An autumn view of Craig Maesglase, which is part of the gentle Dyfi hills situated to the east of Dinas Mawddwy.

Above: The fast flowing Afon Clywedog near Dolgellau, on a damp autumn day.

Opposite: The Afon Clywedog, to the east of Dolgellau, rushes between glistening rocks and gullies. The water is frozen in motion, creating a silky veil.

The Afon Clywedog, which is overlooked from the footpath on the popular Torrent Walk near Dolgellau, snakes its way through woodlands.

A tree silhouetted against the setting sun.

The shapely hill of Carreg-y-saeth
seen across Llyn Cwm Bycan,
situated in the heart of the Rhynog
to the east of Harlech.

An impressive drystone wall snakes its way up the southern ridge of Rhinog Fach.

A steely view across the Y Lethr Slabs and Llyn Hywel to Rhinog Fach and the distant Rhinog Fawr.
Here is to be found some of the wildest and roughest terrain in North Wales.

The Afon Cwmnantcol rushes down a series
of cascades, carrying golden leaves in its path,
towards the village of Llanbedr, situated
just south of Harlech.

Left: An explosion of autumn colours.

Opposite: Rhinog Fawr dominates the
head of Cwm Nantcol.

Orange lichen adds colour to a drystone wall.

The imposing Rhinog Fawr and Rhinog Fach on the skyline seen from the road to Maes-y-garnedd at the head of Cwm Nantcol. The deep cleft between the hills is Bwlch Drws Ardudwy, through which an old drovers' road passed.

A ruined farmhouse in Cwm Nantcol backed by Rhynog Fawr and Rhynog Fach.

Dyffryn burial chamber, a Neolithic
site dating back to 3-4000 BC, in the
village of Dyffryn Ardudwy.

Above: The superb sandy beach at Harlech.

Opposite: A lone boulder acts as a foreground in this view across to the Lleyn Peninsula, from the beach at Llandanwg.

Left: The sand dunes at Harlech lead the eye towards Porthmadog, backed by the shapely peak of Moel Hebog.

Opposite: The last rays of the setting sun touch boulders and add warmth to this view north across Tremadog Bay, from the beach near Llandanwg.

Beautiful contrasts of colour, created by the deciduous and evergreen trees at Minffordd below the southern slopes of Cadair Idris.

The trees enliven this view across the slopes of Craig Llwyd overlooking Minffordd.

One of the many streams tumbling
down the wooded hillside below
Cwm Cau, on the southern
flanks of Cadair Idris.

Llyn Cau, overlooked by spectacular cliffs, is one of the finest cwms in Wales.

A bird's-eye-view of Llyn Cau
from the summit slopes of
Pen y Gadair, the high point
of the Cadair Idris massif.

The craggy summit of Cyfrwy and the distant coast at Barmouth, seen from the summit of Pen y Gadair.

Above: A house shrouded in red foliage on the shore of Llyn Mwyngil at Tal y Llyn.

Opposite: An isolated farm at the foot of Cwm Amarch overlooking Llyn Mwyngil at Tal y Llyn.

Right: The pointed peak of Pared y Cefn-hir overlooking Llyn Cregennen and its boat house.

Opposite: Two types of heather, ling and bell, and the golden flowers of gorse create a colourful foreground of this view above Llyn Cregennen near Arthog, with the Cadair Idris range in the background.

Sunrise across Llyn Cregennen backed by the Cadair Idris range.

Evening light on the northern section of the Cadair Idris range reflected in Llyn Cregennen.

A fiery sunset reflected in the waters of the Afon Mawddach, near Bontddu.

The soft play of evening light picks out the west-facing cliffs of Cadair Idris, in this view across the Afon Mawddach.

Above: An evening view west across the Mawddach Estuary to the Cadair Idris range seen from the rugged hillside of Dinas Oleu, above Barmouth. Dinas Oleu was the first property bequeathed to the National Trust after its foundation in 1895.

Opposite: The last rays of the setting sun light up the mouth of the Mawddach Estuary, and the sand spit of Ro Wen, at Barmouth

An autumn view up to the head of the Valley of the Afon Dysynni (the Dysynni Valley)
to the north-east of Towyn.

The aptly named Craig yr Aderyn (Bird Rock) in the Dysynni Valley, is the haunt of many species of birds including cormorants, which are normally coastal dwellers.

Above: The ruins of Castell y Bere, situated on a rocky mound, in its secluded location at the head of the Dysynni Valley with the Cadair Idris range rising behind it. Built by the warring princes during the thirteenth century, today the ruins are of historical importance.

Opposite: The setting sun highlights the flanks of Cadair Idris at the head of the Dysynni Valley.

Overleaf: The sun sets over the Snowdon hills.